Make A Left On Flightless Lane

Lucy Taylor

Presentation by *BookLeaf Publishing*

Web: www.bookleafpub.com

E-mail: info@bookleafpub.com

ISBN: 9789357440011

First edition 2023

DEDICATION

For those come and gone, for those who stayed,
and those I'll never speak with again. The words
you have printed on my heart, shown here.

ACKNOWLEDGEMENT

Thank you to the full and happy individuals inspiring bright thoughts, ideas, and expression. Thank you to the empty and hateful individuals inspiring pained declarations of what you have done to me. Equally, you fabricate my art.

PREFACE

Poetry, in my opinion, is one of the most beautiful and fruitful means of art and expression. Make A Left On Flightless Lane is my outlet serving the purpose of a release of anger, love, frustration, jealousy, and delight. I do hope you enjoy.

Smiling Eyes

Reopening a door does not guarantee change,
yet the possibility remains.
Chances of scheming souls to reverse from conditional
love,
often a rare occurrence.
They'll encourage the notion of manipulation for better,
and oh how you make me believe.
Your sparks fly, threatening wildfires,
yet I only see the candle in your eyes;
fragrant flames lick the edges of my heart.
They bring a tender warmth,
invite a raw tendency.
And suddenly,
the rise and fall of the sun each day matter so little
because the affliction lessens each evening.
You come with false hope,
though hope nonetheless.
I see the game through stained glass,
which largely brings importance.
Consciously accepting heartache from your lying lips
proves to be the sweetest revenge on those
smiling eyes.

My Meaning

Betrayal.
A familiar gravel road I travel, only by foot.
Patience.
A beautiful wish for many, a reality for few.
Jealousy.
My pretty gifted bow I tie in my hair each day.
Guilt.
The soreness of my scalp when I let down my hair.
Heartache.
The blood running through my veins, and becoming infected.
Contemplation.
A cold stroll in the park, alone.
Togetherness.
The height of a bell tower, the sturdiness of a marble statue.
Decisions.
The early flutter of your eyelids before rising.
Compatibility.
Two legs strapped together, winning a race.
Joy...

Missing Possibility

How do I miss us,
when we never even happened?
Your faint gaze pulls desire from my lips.
"Mine," I whisper.
Your silence brings answers,
and your hands are my comfort.
Letting go the hold of my heart you possess,
and falling back into the match I compete in.
For you,
I play this game.
Entertaining possibilities for yourself,
a blood death match for myself.
A stupid contest with no ultimate results,
for I'll never win your heart.
It belongs to only you,
as mine throbs in your corner.
Cut me from the group;
this was never a team sport.

Oh Sweetness

I want your silk skin on mine,
and oh how I yearn to taste your sweetness.
Our passion of love burns fires on my legs,
and tickles up my spine.
Your power,
my encouragement.
I dream this reality will surface,
bubble over,
for a gentle release.
Oh sweetness,
come see what you do to me.

Facing Serenity

Life; rhythm in my words
and throughout the designs.
She is apprehension, a grasp of that knot in my head,
her idle fingers untwisting.
A talk of pain, regret;
yet I feel glad.
Glad and grateful
in her sunbeams of color;
a rainbow of one line.
Followed to conclusion,
it slows the heart
facing serenity.
A heaviness she separates me from,
and I'll leave it in that office trash can.

Hole In The Drywall

It's not funny;
your eyes and my mouth,
they lock and find
jealousy.
Picture sweet grapes,
the wink of a cat,
my bliss of sight.
The blessings we have been given,
and how you are a part of them.
No matter the lessons you've taught,
I feel anger;
I will always feel anger.
Apologies are no cure for
the damage you've done.

Clone Off Their Block

I love your defense of the
things that hurt me most,
and the advocacy
for everyone but me.
Your stupid million dollar smile,
all people see;
you will find that none
of these eyes are on me.
Protection of the terrible,
tear down of the weak,
I'll see you supporting
only your little clique.
I yearn for payback
from the greed,
I wish would occur
with faster speed.

I Wish I Were A Coaster

I want to be a coaster,
but instead,
I am me.
The daily heartache,
a subscription I don't even pay for;
it arrives promptly,
every day.
I feel
time is my anxiety,
and speed is my bliss.
Give me a break,
Grandfather.
Your clock ticks,
and I listen.
Do you know something
that can't listen?
A coaster.

Flowers And Jelly Beans

Flavor and scent.
A pea and its pair.
Pretend and hope;
it can be found anywhere,
only if there is connection.
Believe to find truth,
and not giving up what we have earned, built.
Surfing on the shore is
me not loving you,
a fish caught.
A locked gaze,
light fingers.
Children,
and the innocent romance.
Beauty and pain
in art,
and all around.
Favorites and dislikes I see,
beauty floating around
nevertheless.
Long, flowy hair,
and your eyelashes fluttering
below a shy grin.
Charming elegance overall,
I seek in the
touch of our flowers,
and the tender bite of a
jellybean.

Dizzy

To strike a metal,
it may be overrated.
Copper means close to
zero,
while silver gets you
little.
Gold.
What everyone wants, and few obtain.
While fighting for any,
most get none.
While fighting for any,
you lose all the fun.
While fighting for any,
we fail and fail;
we call it a simple challenge, a task for our thoughts.
Those achieving,
given the world we provide.
Broken and crushed,
every morsel goes to the
Gold.
This cruel arrangement we throw ourselves in to go
around and around.
Mindless circles;
I am dizzy.

Annie

You drive me wild;
wild as the bursting orange sunset,
reflecting off your eyes.
I say,
"I love you. Always."
and you smile in return.
I know regardless if spoken,
you feel the same.
Looking out, trees expanding above
petite flowers brushing their base.
But a tiny undertone, of the
joy you bring.
Without you, well.
I can't even imagine.

Puzzlement

Is there much to be withheld,
or any?
Do I assume love,
when none is present?
Or maybe it is;
the signals turn positive.
Your ease of life brings such enrichment to me,
and if the light should ever turn green,
I will be the first to go.
To cross the finish line,
and claim the prize that has always been mine.
The trophy of you,
the past,
and the mansion of our eternal inclination.

Living The Nightmare

Black dreams,
and rather, I go back every morning.
A terror; horror
depicting some depth of my reality.
Oh, the hidden connections,
and who, but you, to blame.
It's as listening to the best part of a song,
not even knowing the rest.
With time, the rest becomes learned.
You find you love it equally.
But my music has been on pause,
and I just can't seem to find the play button.
You hid it,
with whatever control you possess.
And if dark circles and falling eyelids mean freedom,
I will live this shortening,
worsening
nightmare.

Languages Of Love

It has remained,
and always will be,
just so right to love; to care.
I think about the time in my life,
how I live every day and the end lays ahead.
A heartache,
a headache,
and everything in between,
Your kindness to a loved one,
and repayment in a different language.
They'll show or tell you,
and such a wonderful performance will go on.
A matching token of connection, perhaps,
and a sweet word of admiration.
The beauty in small and large productions of truth,
and the realness each of them hold.
A fondness of an individual carrying such depth,
you promise them.
A swear kept while crossing the heart like a bridge,
and the genuine lovers never grow tired of the
same old,
magnificent view.

Envy

I envy children,
for they are ignorant.
Their realizations have yet to take place,
when I will envy them no longer.
It isn't jealousy, as I can admit
the presence of violence.
I want to kill and hunt my predators until they beg
I take mercy on their pathetic lives.
A bullet through the head they deserve,
and hope they'll get.
A drawing to hurt,
because they hurt me first.

A Wreck Of The Faithful

Death is my looming factor,
and he seems to pick victims so randomly.
The kindness of a smile does not sway
the grasp of his neck or the limp in his walk.
A shudder down his spine,
and the sour pinch in a breath of air.
It will be taken from me,
and is edging away with others.
Oh my,
his will.
The pure, strong eyes soaking in candy showers,
yet walking in alone.
How brave.

WODO

I will drink this soda,
and I will pet my cat.
I will smile at spineless cruelty and ignore the lips they
come from.
I will do everything I do desire,
because he did it first.
I saw his passion for pleasure,
and how he fulfilled it every day.
What he loved,
brought to life in the face of impossibility;
he did it.
He lived through the brush nearly ending him,
as we live every day.
We only die once.

I Love My Twin

A softness and reality; I saw it.
He, who held a brave face above dark clouds,
and never let those thunderstorms turn to tears.
A sense of power so strong,
yet it couldn't mask the despair of a counterpart so near.
But far or close,
his love shown in jaded procedures ran high.
He is frightened.
Frightened for his proximity in connection,
and the quickening possibilities.
I can picture the angered footsteps,
and the brew of thoughts in his mind that brought them
about.
How I knew he'd kill the one who started it all,
all in the most torturous way.
He has much to speak,
but may never mourn the unfeasible truth of death.
The card game taken a harsh turn,
only to take another abruptly.
His hand was nearly played.

Hate You

I draw and erase you.
I do it over and over again.
I remove you from my past and I kick you out of my future.
It helps reflected insecurity;
forgiveness to myself.
Why I ever let you blame me for crimes you committed
upon my soul.
It is scarred and cut,
with conflicting messages.
The desire for distance,
yet the need for an apology;
it is so compelling.
Your handprints erase from my skin with hours and days,
but somehow reappear with moments and nights.
How lies can burn me eternally;
you must be already charred.

Mister Unlucky

I was irrelevant enough to be shut out,
when the closeness is so far,
a barrier is formed.
By you, the hurt;
and I, the unwanted help.
It's a hit unwelcomed,
yet I was never wanted before.
Accepted yet rejected,
I have no say in their response,
unless I prevent it.
Your kindly dislike makes me embarrassed for the effort
I give
with nothing expected in return.
And it is nothing that I get.
Empty gifts to you,
my whole heart to me.
The careless meet the caring,
to mix up a drink of remiss and despair.

Reminiscing You

Abandoned yet left,
she never understood the laughs you gave.
The way I heard your stories,
and intentions from the untouched.
A dark black sky,
the stars through the hallway of your time,
and shivering from the frigid.
Your final words,
hanging in the air;
you left me there.
On a flight crossing the world of life,
I don't have your guidance.
How much you are missed,
the love I still push,
your remembrance.
Your heavenly body I still see each night
and when I wake;
the presence of you remains.